Newcastle
City Council

Newcastle Libraries and Information Service

 **0845 002 0336**

12\07

Due for return	Due for return	Due for return

Please return this item to any of Newcastle's Libraries by the last date shown above. If not requested by another customer the loan can be renewed, you can do this by phone, post or in person.
Charges may be made for late returns.

Family Memories

When Your Gran Was Little

Jane Bidder

Illustrated by Shelagh McNicholas

W

FRANKLIN WATTS
LONDON•SYDNEY

For my mother, Sally, my mother-in-law, Dot,
and all grandmothers everywhere − J.B.

To Moya, Chris and Trisha − S.M.

The author and publisher wish to thank everyone who contributed their memories to this book.

This edition 2007
First published in 2004 by Franklin Watts
338 Euston Road, London NW1 3BH

Franklin Watts Australia
Level 17/207 Kent Street, Sydney, NSW 2000

Text © Jane Bidder 2004
Illustrations © Franklin Watts 2004

Editor: Caryn Jenner
Designer: James Marks
Art director: Jonathan Hair
Picture research: Diana Morris
Photography: Ray Moller unless otherwise credited.

Picture credits: Advertising Archives: 20. Lindsay Hebberd/Corbis: front cover tl, 12. Picturepoint/Topham: front cover clb, 7, 11, 14, 19, 22, 24, 28cl, 28tr. Science Museum, London/Topham: front cover cla, 16.

Every attempt has been made to clear copyright. Should there be any inadvertent omission please apply to the publisher for rectification.

A CIP catalogue record for this book is available from the British Library.

ISBN 978-0-7496-7812-8

Printed in China

Franklin Watts is a division of Hachette Children's Books, an Hachette Livre UK Company.

Contents

Changing times

These pictures show children in the present and in the past.

You are growing up in the present.

Present
This is a picture of a family in the present. ▼

Your gran grew up in the past. Many things have changed since your gran was a child.

In this book, lots of different grandmothers remember what it was like when they were your age.

▲ Past
This is a picture of a family in the past. The picture was taken in 1952.

Coal fire

"When I was little, my father used to bring coal in from the shed to make a fire. The coal fire kept us warm and cosy, but we couldn't sit too close or we'd get burnt."

Gathering round a coal fire was a popular way to spend a cold winter evening. You could even toast bread in the fire with a special long fork.

Ration book

"When I was little, the war had just ended. There wasn't enough food for everyone, so we had ration books to show how much we could buy at the shops. Once we used up our rations, we had to wait for more."

Oh dear, this is the last of our sugar rations.

You'll have to make it last until next month.

The shopkeeper ticked the box in the ration book to show what had been bought. In some ration books, the shopkeeper ripped out a little token.

11

Making dolls

"When I was little, I lived in Africa. My sisters and I used to make our own dolls using leftover fabric and beads. My favourite doll was called Swazi. She came everywhere with me."

In the 1940s and 1950s, children often made their own toys. These dolls are from South Africa.

The Coronation

"When I was little, we watched the Coronation of Queen Elizabeth on our neighbours' TV. They had the only TV on the street, so we all went there to have a party!"

Queen Elizabeth officially became Queen of England at her Coronation, which took place in 1953.

Washing mangle

"When I was little, my mum and I used to wring out the washing with a mangle. Mum put the wet clothes between the rollers, then she let me turn the handle to squeeze out the water."

This mangle from 1948 has a tub built in to catch the water. Modern washing machines have a spin cycle to wring out the wet washing.

School playground

"When I was little, my school had a rule that girls and boys had to play on different sides of the playground. Sometimes I wanted to play football with the boys, but Miss wouldn't let me."

You're not allowed on the boys' playground, Jean.

But why, Miss? I want to play football.

At some schools, girls and boys played together. These children are twirling plastic hula hoops. The hula hoop was a very popular toy in the 1950s.

19

Liberty bodice

"When I was little, my mum took me to the shop to buy a Liberty bodice. I wore it under my clothes, with wool stockings. To hold up the stockings, I had a suspender belt with hooks."

A Liberty bodice was warm and soft to wear under a dress or blouse.

Flower game

"When I was little, I lived in Malaysia. My friends and I used to play a game with a kind of ball made with flowers. We kicked the ball to each other and tried not to let it touch the ground."

The ball was made with frangipane flowers. A leaf or stem was used to tie the petals together.

Telegrams

"When I was little, a telegram boy came to the house and gave my mum a message on a piece of paper. It said that Aunty May had had a baby boy! We didn't have a telephone, so she had sent us a telegram instead."

A telegraph operator typed out the message, then gave it to the telegram boy to deliver.

Bedtime

"When I was little, my gran tucked me into bed at night. We used to read a story together, then she kissed me goodnight and turned out the light. Now that I'm a granny, I like to read bedtime stories with my granddaughter."

Timeline

This timeline shows the years from 1945 to 2010.

1945

1950

1960

The grans in this book were children during the 1940s and 1950s.

1970

During the 1960s and 1970s, these grans became mums. This is when your mum and dad were probably children.

1980

1990

2000

2010

You are a child now. What year were you born? When do you think you will be grown up?

Memories

Ask your gran about when she was a child. Ask your teachers and other grown-ups about their memories, too.

Here are some questions to ask.

What were your favourite toys and games?

What kinds of clothes did you wear?

What special events do you remember?

What things do we have now that you didn't have when you were a child?

How was your school different from mine?

Glossary

Memories   Things you remember from the past.
Do you have *memories* of your last birthday?

Remember   To think of the past.
Do you *remember* what you did yesterday?

Past   Time gone by. The *past* can mean yesterday or it can mean a long time ago. Your gran was a child in the *past*.

Present   Now. Today is in the *present*.
You are a child in the *present*.

Timeline   A chart that shows the passing of time.
See the *timeline* on page 28.

Index